Flies in the Water,
Fish in the Air

Also by Jim Arnosky

Deer at the Brook
Drawing from Nature
Drawing Life in Motion
Freshwater Fish & Fishing
Secrets of a Wildlife Watcher.
Watching Foxes

LOTHROP, LEE & SHEPARD BOOKS | NEW YORK

FLIES IN THE WATER, FISH IN THE AIR

A Personal Introduction to Fly Fishing
by artist and naturalist
JIM ARNOSKY

To Merle Dailey,
for all the times
we've met at the water

Library of Congress Cataloging in
Publication Data

Arnosky, Jim.
Flies in the water, fish in the air.

Includes index.
Summary: An anecdotal account of the
pleasures of fly fishing, discussing the
choice and use of tackle, kinds of flies,
walking in water, and watching for fish.
1. Fly fishing. [1. Fly fishing] I. Title.
SH456.A76   1986   799.1'2   84-29684
ISBN 0-688-05834-5

Typography by Lynn Braswell

This book is a personal introduction, pure and simple, to fly fishing. It is written from my own knowledge and experiences and only hints at all there is for you to know, learn, and enjoy about this wonderful subject.

Jim Arnosky
Ramtails 1986

Contents

1
Insects and Fish

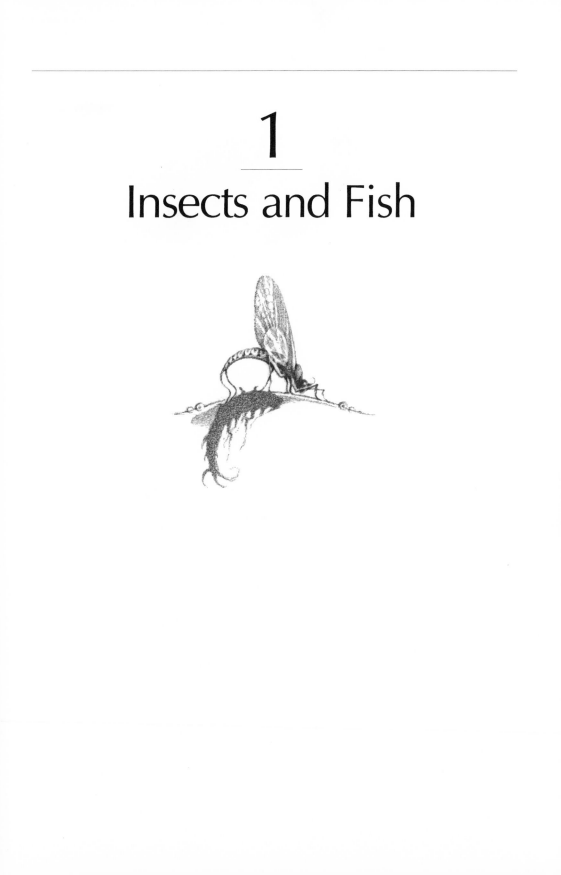

It had been raining for days and now it was clearing off. A great mass of dry air from the northwest was pushing the last of the rain clouds to the east. The clearing winds whipped the pond, making the surface rough and choppy. Small waves licked the shore where I stood, wondering if trying to cast a dry-fly into such waters would be worth the effort.

Keeping my sight within the range of casting possibilities, I scanned the water wave by wave looking for an encouraging sign that fish were feeding on the surface—a slap, a splash, or a swirl. I saw the next best thing. A large yellow mayfly was floating on the water. As I watched, the fly took flight and I trained my eyes on its opaque wings as it rose steadily in the blustery air and flew away toward the opposite shore. I searched the waves again, where I had first noticed the mayfly, and saw more. They were all similar in size and color to the first. Some were floating on the water. Some were lifting off in flight. I wondered if the fish in the pond were perhaps feeding underwater on the emerging flies. Then suddenly a large bronze-sided bass shot up and out of the water after one of the airborne flies. The big fish jumped with such gusto it continued up through the air for well over two feet, presumably with fly in mouth, its tail still wiggling in a swimming motion. The silly look of it made me laugh aloud. Abruptly, gravity brought the "flight" to a halt, and the bass fell back to the water and belly flopped heavily into the pond.

The sight was more than encouraging. It was downright stimulating! I tied on a fly of my own, similar in color and size to the mayflies in the water, and tested the knot with a tug equal to one I imagined the bass I had just seen could give, then waded into the pond to make my cast.

MAYFLIES

Whenever I think of jumping fish, I also think of mayflies. They are the insects most often associated with fly fishing, especially fly fishing for trout. Mayflies live in a variety of water types, from still to slow-moving to fast. They have slender segmented abdomens and very fine long tails. Every mayfly has four wings—two large ones and two smaller. At rest, all four wings are held upright and clasped together. In this position the four wings appear to be one wing, and on the water can resemble a sail on a boat.

Mayflies come in a variety of sizes and colors. Each color or combination of colors marks a different type. I have seen white, gray, black, tan, brown, yellow, green, olive, and pink mayflies. Some species are genuine mayfly giants with wings that stand over an inch tall. Other mayfly species

MAYFLY

AT REST

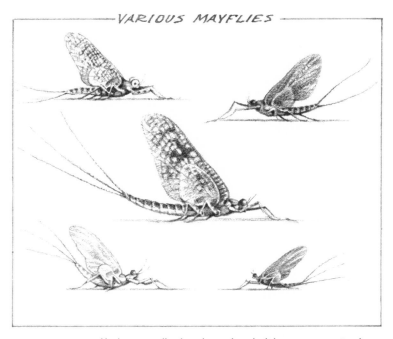

VARIOUS MAYFLIES

are so small that in flight they look like gnats. Only when they alight do their sail-like wings tell you they are mayflies. I was fishing in our river in a drizzling rain when a little fly alighted on the back of my rod hand. It was a tiny mayfly with upright wings no higher than a quarter of an inch. I carefully lifted my hand to my face for a closer look. The mayfly's wings were blue-gray. Its slender little body was olive green. Before my eyes the tiny creature slowly flexed its wings down once and up again. In the soft light of the rainy day, the motion was absolutely lovely.

Mayflies actually live most of their lives underwater, beginning as eggs that hatch into "nymphs." Mayfly nymphs are durable little creatures. They have an outer skeleton of "chitin"— the same material that armors crabs and lobsters. Some nymphs cling to submerged rocks, and others crawl or swim along the bottom. There are also nymphs that burrow into silt, or mud. All are important fish food, rich in protein. Many of the trout I catch and clean have stomachs packed full of nymphs. The nymphs themselves eat minute particles of vegetation. The nymphal stage of most mayfly species lasts about one year. I have collected mayfly nymphs from our brook in the dead of winter, when the water was running under its own frozen surface and blanketed by deep snow. Every time a nymph outgrows its chitin, it molts and the nymph begins a new phase of growth in fresh new chitin. Each shed chitin is called a "shuck." The growing period from one molt to the next is called an "instar."

There comes an instar in every nymph's life when the insect reaches full growth and is ready to change from nymphal form into a winged fly. When this happens, the nymph ventures into open water. Migrating nymphs are vulnerable and fish will eat every one they can catch. Depending upon their species, the nymphs will shed their last nymphal shuck while on the bottom and then swim to the surface as winged mayflies; crawl out

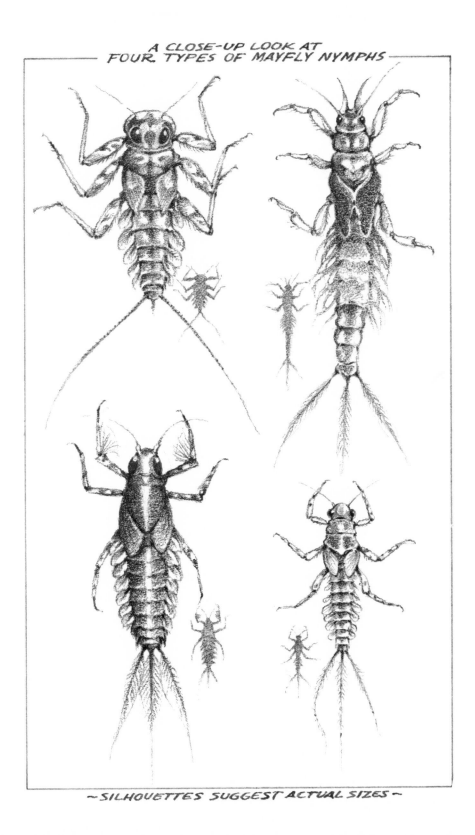

~ SILHOUETTES SUGGEST ACTUAL SIZES ~

EMERGING
DUN

(WINGS STILL
UNFOLDING)

NYMPH
SWIMMING UP
TO THE SURFACE

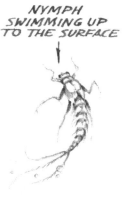

of the water as nymphs and then molt; or swim to the surface, evacuating their nymphal shucks along the way. However it is done, the physical transformation from nymphs to winged flies is known in fly fishing as the "hatch." It is not really a hatch, but the *emergence* of adult flies; and all during it fish feed.

A newly emerged mayfly is called a "dun," after the gray color of its new wings. Duns cannot fly right away. Their wings, freshly pulled out of their nymphal shucks, are still too wet. While the duns float on the water's surface waiting for their wings to dry, fish need only rise and gulp them down. I once saw a mayfly dun using its own floating nymphal shuck as a raft to stand on while its wings dried. The moment the dun lifted off in flight, a small bass rose and gulped, getting only the shuck as the fly flew away. At best, mayfly duns are slow fliers. Often, fish will jump right out of the water and snatch them from the air. Other predators also catch and eat mayflies. Bats and birds take their share. Duns that escape these hungry feeders fly directly to shoreline vegetation and alight—if they haven't gotten caught in any spider webs—on sheltered leaves or twigs. Here they rest in comparative safety for hours, while they await the fourth and final stage of their lives.

The mayflies molt once more, this time emerging as sexually mature "spinners." Mayfly spinners are exquisite polished versions of the duns. Spinners are more slender and delicately formed. Where the dun body was pale in color, the spinner's body is vivid. Gone are the opaque dun gray wings. Spinners have clear translucent wings that are glisteningly veined. But their beauty is short-lived. Spinners last only long enough to mate.

Spinners fly rapidly, rising and dropping repeatedly in the air. It is this flight behavior for which they are named. I have my own reason for their name. Just trying to focus on one in the air can make your head spin. The males and females swarm over water, pair off, then mate in flight. While mating, the female does the flying while the male fertilizes her eggs. Then they separate and the female deposits the eggs into the water. Some types of mayflies drop their eggs en masse as they fly over the water. More commonly seen are those spinners that deposit their eggs by diving down and dipping their eggs again and again into the water's surface until all have been washed off. Once deposited, the eggs sink to the bottom, where eventually they will hatch into nymphs, continuing the cycle.

Having performed the act of reproduction, all the spinners fall to the water, exhausted. They float on the surface, wings prone. Their lives are spent. There is nothing left for them to do but die. This "spinner fall" is another feeding opportunity for

FEMALE
WITH
EGG-MASS

fish. But since there is little left in the worn-out bodies of the mayflies, it takes many more of them to make a full belly. Fish feeding on fallen spinners stay up near the surface, taking fly after fly, until their mouths are full. Then they retreat to the bottom to swallow it all.

CADDISFLIES

CADDISFLY

Another insect nearly as popular with hungry fish as the mayfly is the caddisfly. Caddisflies are close relatives of moths, but—unlike moths, and much like mayflies—caddisflies live most of their lives underwater.

CADDIS WORMS

I first became aware of them while cleaning a small stream on our property. As I removed fallen tree branches and rotting leaves so the stream could flow more freely, I discovered small cylindrical tubes littering the stream's pebbly bottom. Upon examining one, I found it to be a hollow case made of tiny pebbles with something alive inside. That something was a caddisfly larva, and the tube, called a "caddis case," was its home.

The life cycle of a caddisfly follows: egg, larva (worm), pupa, and then winged adult. Although there may be a thousand different species of caddisflies in North America, on the whole they can be separated into two groups—those who, as worms, live "naked" and those who build cases to live in. Both types are important as fish food. Because the case-building types are more obvious in the water, I am more familiar with them. The kind of case a caddis worm makes depends upon the species of caddis it happens to be. Some build cylindrical cases out of tiny pebbles. Others construct simpler odd-shaped pebble cases. There are caddis worms that build rustic-looking cases out of sticks and leaf matter. All materials used in caddis cases are held together with silk produced by the worms themselves.

My favorite type of caddis case is one made out of tiny cut strands of leaf. The worms that make them carefully wrap the strands in a way that creates a tapered rectangular tube. The workmanship in these particular caddis cases is remarkable.

A caddis worm's case provides protection and camouflage in a stream environment. A caddis worm can move about in search of food while dragging its case along. When danger threatens, the worm retreats inside.

If you live near a shallow, slow-moving stream, look for caddis cases. Where you find one, you are sure to find more. Often caddis worms attach their cases to something stable in the current. Submerged rocks and boulders, drowned branches, and sunken tree trunks are favored. Each caddis worm attaches its case so that the front opening

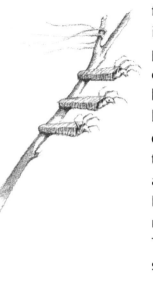

faces the current. Then the worm hangs out, with its legs outstretched, waiting to grab minute food particles—usually vegetation—that drift by. It is common to find many caddis cases stationed side by side, all sharing the current's gifts of food. I have fished in streams where it seemed every boulder had a caddis settlement stuck to it. These settlements remind me of trailer parks; all the cases are uniform in size and style, neatly spaced apart. Every one faces the same direction, into the current. Trout pick caddis cases off boulders and logs. They also catch those cases that are drifting downstream, having been knocked loose. Fish eat both worm and case.

After living through a winter, a caddis worm makes a cocoon (inside its case, if it has one), within which it transforms into a pupa. When the pupa is ready to emerge, it cuts its way out of the cocoon, usually at dusk or night, and swims up to the water's surface. During this swim, the pupa is most vulnerable, and fish take the advantage. I have caught some of my largest fish using small flies tied to imitate swimming caddis pupae. Many caddis pupae migrating to the surface at once can trigger the fish into a feeding spree.

Some types of caddisflies climb out of the water as pupae, then shed their pupal skins to emerge as winged adults. Other caddisflies evacuate their pupal skins and emerge while floating on the

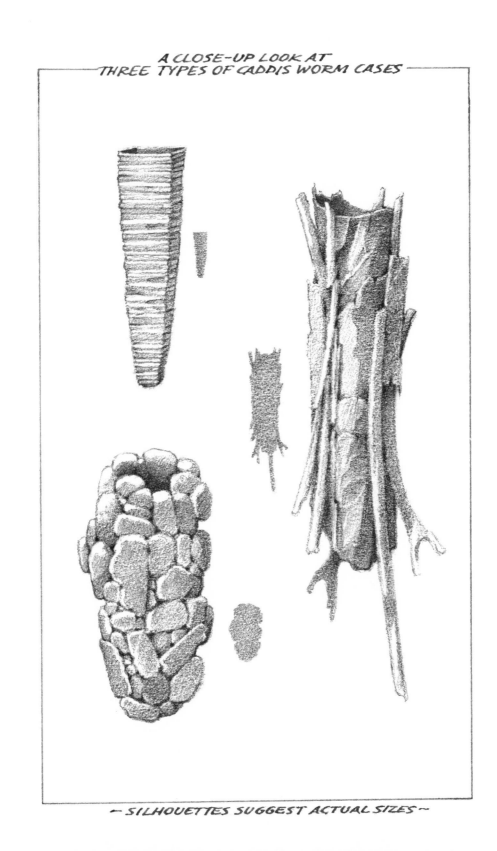

PUPA

water's surface. There always are a percentage of caddisflies that cannot get completely out of their pupal skins. As they struggle to emerge, eager fish gobble them down.

Adult caddisflies have opaque wings covered with minute hairs. At rest, the wings are held in a tent shape over the flies' backs. Though there are numerous species of caddisflies in North America, I have only seen three different-looking types— those with black or gray wings approximately half an inch long, those with uniformly brown wings a little over half an inch long, and those with mottled brown wings nearly an inch long.

Once emerged, adult caddisflies are off and flying in a hurry. They mate on shore. Then the females return to the water and deposit their eggs. The eggs may be attached to vegetation hanging over the water, into which the hatching worms will fall. Or the females actually dive in and deposit their eggs on or under water. If they aren't caught in mid-dive by fish, the caddisflies fly to shore areas to live out the rest of their days. Adult caddisflies can live a month or more. When death finally draws near, the flies return to the water and fall, spent, to the surface. The fish, as always, are on hand to clean up.

STONEFLIES

Stoneflies are aptly named. Cold fast-moving free-stone streams are stonefly havens. The most obvious sign that stoneflies live in a stream is the occasional presence, during summer, of empty nymphal shucks left clinging to streamside boulders.

A stonefly begins life as an egg, hatches into a nymph, then emerges as a winged adult. The bulk of its lifetime, which can be as long as three years in some species, is lived underwater. By now you must have guessed that this characteristic is shared by all of the insects that are most important as food for fish.

STONEFLY

EMPTY NYMPHAL SHUCKS

Stonefly nymphs look a little bit like mayfly nymphs, but they are generally huskier and have more coarsely featured chitin coverings. They each have two whiplike tails, and the undersides of their bodies are lighter in color than their topsides. Some species of stonefly nymphs are very small, less than half an inch long. Others are more than two inches long. These are the largest insects regularly eaten by trout. One of them is something a trout can really sink its teeth into.

Stonefly nymphs spend much of their time creeping under stones. If they accidentally lose hold of the stream bottom, they can become helplessly caught in the current. Fish need only face into the current and swallow nymphs that tumble downstream to them.

Each time a stonefly nymph outgrows its chitin, it molts and begins a new instar. When finished growing as a nymph, it is ready to emerge and make that perilous swim to the surface. Often stonefly nymphs mature in numbers and migrate together to the surface. They crawl out of the water in groups, congregating on dry rocks or shoreline, where they emerge as adult flies. This is when they leave the exposed empty nymphal shucks mentioned earlier. Whenever I see such congregations of shucks, I tie on a nymph pattern of my own and fish it along the bottom, hoping the trout haven't already had their fill.

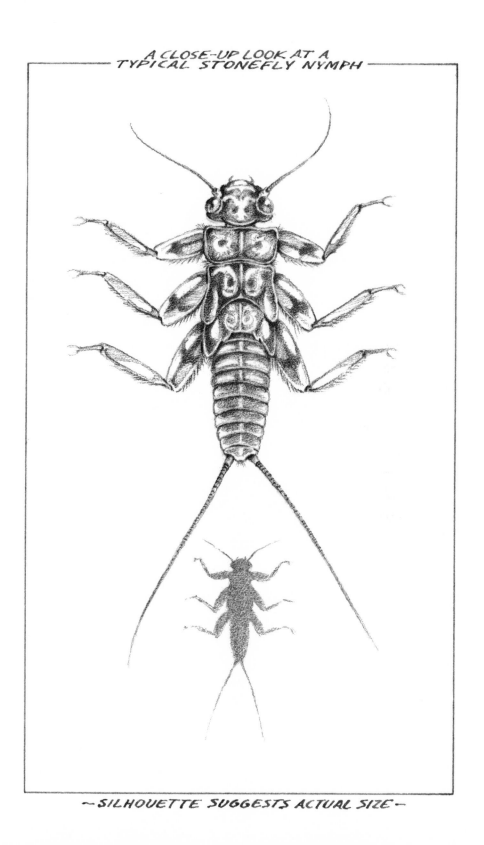

~ SILHOUETTE SUGGESTS ACTUAL SIZE ~

STONEFLY
IN FLIGHT

Over the years, I have seen yellow stoneflies, tan stoneflies, reddish stoneflies, and dark brown stoneflies, at different hours of the day. Adult stoneflies have four shiny wings. When they are flying, you can see all four. At rest, stoneflies hold their wings flat, on top of each other, on their backs. Males are noticeably smaller than females of the same species.

When a male emerges, it locates a mate. After mating, females deposit their eggs in the water by dropping them en masse, by floating on the surface and letting the water wash the eggs off, or by skipping over the water and dipping the eggs into it. No matter which method is used, while the females are depositing their eggs, their predominant wings keep beating.

STONEFLY
AT REST

MOSQUITOS, GNATS, AND MIDGES

Whenever I see fish obviously feeding on the surface but cannot tell what they are eating no matter
how I strain my eyes to see, I assume they are
feeding on mosquitos, gnats, or midges. I have
mixed feelings about these minute insects. It's exciting to know the fish are actively feeding on
something, and the challenge of trying to cast and
fish the tiny tied flies that imitate such bugs is en-
joyable. But since this particular insect group includes some of the nasty biting bugs, I fear that
while the fish feed on the insects, the insects will
feed on me.

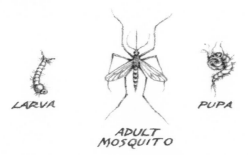

LARVA

PUPA

ADULT
MOSQUITO

Mosquitos, gnats, and midges are related insects. They look similar and have the same life cy-
cles, beginning their lives as eggs, hatching into
larvae, pupating, and then emerging as winged
adults. Fish eat the larvae, pupae, and adults. Sur-
prisingly large fish will feed on these tiny insects. I

EMERGING MIDGES

have watched rainbow trout rolling on the surface as they fed exclusively on gnats that were nearly invisible. It's not surprising to learn that a lot of these small flies are needed for a meal. So the fish feed steadily, taking bug after bug. A really big fish that lingers near the surface to do this—its wide dorsal fin waving out of the water—can drive a fisherman to extremes. For just such extreme times, I carry a selection of flies sparsely tied on hooks so small you have to cross your eyes to see them. For when fish are feeding on these minute insects, they simply shun any other fly, real or artificial, that is too large.

TERRESTRIALS

"Terrestrial" is a name fly fishermen use for an insect that normally does not live in water but sometimes falls in accidentally. Ants, beetles, caterpillars, crickets, grasshoppers, hornets, and bees are all landlubbers that occasionally find themselves in the soup. Fish strike terrestrials with a savage enthusiasm. I was once fishing a section of a stream where the water funneled through a V-shaped ledge formation. It looked trouty to me. There were some hanging branches over the water. I decided to try fishing a small black ant pattern, casting it to look as if a real ant had fallen off one of the overhanging branches into the water. This I did. Before I could congratulate myself for having such an ingenious strategy, a large brown trout attacked my ant. The fish struck so viciously, I jerked my rod back too hard. The fish's golden body arced underwater, broke my fine leader tip, and got away with the fly.

Whenever you see a terrestrial fall on the water, watch it. Notice how particular insects behave in their unwanted situation. Remember those that struggle or panic, those that hop or skitter in the water, and those that simply float motionlessly. Then imitate the different actions with the terrestrial fly you choose to fish.

When watching animals struggling for life, it can be hard not to try to help. Once I actually became involved with a bumblebee that was caught floating on the surface of a stream. I didn't see how it got there, but the bee was obviously struggling and in trouble. As it floated downstream, a small fish twice tried to grab it from below. One of the fish's tries pulled the bee under and for an instant it disappeared, suddenly popping up to the surface again. The bee continued downstream toward a spot where a good-sized trout had been surface feeding earlier. I watched to see if the bee would pass over the trout, and if the trout would jump after it. Then some quirk in the current floated the bee off course and into a quiet eddy near the stream bank. I felt guilty about my cold-hearted desire to see the trout nab the bee and decided to go to its rescue.

The bumblebee eagerly climbed out of the water onto my offered rod tip and then, just as eagerly, climbed off the rod onto a smooth dry rock. The hair on its body was completely soaked and matted from being pulled under by the small fish. One of its wings was torn at the end. The bee began drying its head and antennae by rubbing them with its forelegs. I knelt down to get a closer look. For the longest time the bee seemed intent only on drying its head and antennae, even though it looked to me as if its wings were much wetter. They were also stuck together and flat down on the bee's black-and-yellow back. I became impatient to see the wings dried and decided to dry them myself. Moving my face to within a few inches of the bumblebee, I began blowing gently on its wings. They were really wet! I blew and blew. At one point I realized how I would look to someone passing by and began to feel a little foolish. Then, finally, I had blown the bee's wings dry. They became unstuck from each other and stood up off the bee's back. The one that was torn looked much better dry. I could see no reason why the bee wouldn't be able to fly again. So I left it on the rock, still fiddling around with its antennae, and resumed fishing.

2

Choosing and Using Fly-Fishing Equipment

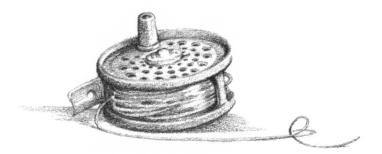

Every so often I treat myself to a day of fishing at my favorite beaver pond. The water here fills a wide bowl of land rimmed on one side by swamp and on the other by the beavers' dam. In the center of the pond, sticking up out of the water, is the beavers' lodge. The area is surrounded by forested mountains and the whole scene is domed by a spectacular expanse of sky. The fish in the pond are native brook trout. Any little disturbance on the water sends these wary fish darting for cover. It takes a light touch to cast a fly to one without spooking it.

One day I was doing all the right things. My casts were skillful. My leader was fine enough to be invisible to the trout. I caught fish after fish. Every little trout I caught and released left some of its wildness and beauty with me. There is nothing more wild and few things as beautiful as a native brook trout.

As I was making one cast, I saw a doe on the other side of the pond, looking in my direction. The deer was standing knee-deep in the grassy water. Her coat was red-brown and the white patch of fur on her throat stood out against the dark woods behind her. At first I thought she was seeing me. Then I realized she was only watching the yellow fly line looping back and forth in the air over my head, because when I ended my cast, the deer looked away.

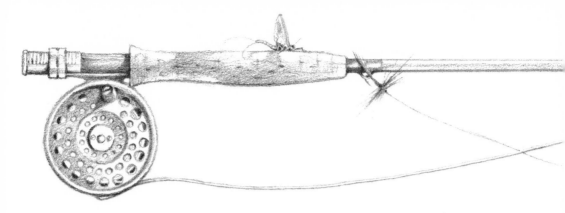

FLY LINES

The plastic-coated fly line is the heart of the fly fishing technique. It is the essential tool that makes it possible to cast a nearly weightless fly long distances over water—for, in fact, it is actually the heavy plastic line that you cast. The fly simply goes along for the ride.

Fly lines come in different weights, each designed to properly cast a spectrum of fly sizes. The heaviest-weight line is a 12-weight line. It can cast the biggest, bushiest, most wind-resistant flies that can be tied. The fly line weights are progressively lighter, from No. 12 through Nos. 11, 10, 9, 8, 7, 6, 5, 4, 3, and 2. The four lightest line weights are designed for delicate fishing involving very fine tippets and tiny flies. All the line weights can be used for big fish. In skillful hands, even a No. 2 line used with a complementary light rod can handle a bully of a trout. But to begin your fishing, you needn't learn all the nuances of different line weights. You can achieve a happy medium by

LEVEL LINE

DOUBLE TAPER

WEIGHT FORWARD

TO REEL

using a 6-weight line. A No. 6 line can cast everything from trout flies to bass bugs. I do much of my fishing for bluegills, perch, trout, and bass with a 6-weight fly line and a rod designed for use with the No. 6 line. (For heavier lines you must also use heavier rods.)

Within the weight category of each line, there is also a choice of tapers. You can buy a 6-weight fly line that is "level," which means it is the same thickness from end to end. But for ease in casting, tapered lines are the thing. For instance, a "double taper" line is thinner at both ends and fatter, for fifteen feet or so, in its middle. This fat "belly" in the line provides a concentration of weight that helps pull more of the line out for distance during a cast. Double taper lines land gently on the water, causing little or no splash that could spook fish. For this reason some fly fishers prefer them. I prefer using a weight forward line. A "weight forward" line is tapered in a way that concentrates (or bellies) most of its weight in the front third of its length. A weight forward line is the easiest to cast, even directly into a wind. The weight in the forward section "shoots" the line out and pushes it through any air resistance.

Alas, we are not through selecting our No. 6 fly line yet. There is also the choice of density to be made. Wait! Don't run off. I simply mean—do we want our line to sink or to float? Either a full sinking line or a sinking tip line is best for fishing flies down ten feet deep or more. I can think of only a few lakes where I fish that would call for a sinking line to get down where the fish stay. For all other situations, I find a floating line is best. A floating line floats because during its manufacture, its plastic coating has been injected with microscopic air bubbles. They keep the line up on the surface and make it possible to float a dry fly on the water. A floating line, used when fishing with a sunken fly, makes it possible for you to watch the line's tip for any sign of a strike. Floating lines are also easier than sinking lines to lift from the water in order to begin a fresh cast.

I use a weight forward No. 6 floating line for nearly all of my fishing. It is a pretty pastel yellow, bright enough to see on the water even after sundown, yet natural enough to be pleasing. When fishing for spooky mountain brookies where everything around the stream is earth brown or forest green, I use a dark amber-colored line that blends with the surroundings. Fly lines also come in browns, greens, oranges, blues, and whites. You can choose whatever color suits you.

TO REEL

BACKUP LINE

SINCE MOST FLY LINES ARE ONLY AROUND 30 YDS. LONG, PUT AT LEAST 25 YDS. OF 20 lb. BRAIDED NYLON LINE ON YOUR REEL FIRST TO SERVE AS A BACKUP LINE.

KNOT

FLY LINE

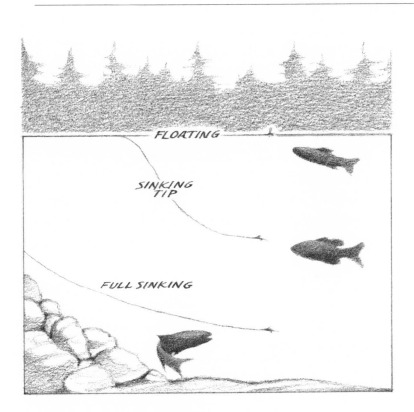

LEADERS AND TIPPETS

Once you have a fly line in hand, it will be obvious that you wouldn't tie a fly directly to it. The terminal tip of a floating or sinking fly line is much too thick to push through the eyelets of most hooks. Even if you could, your fly would look more like a dinghy on a rope than an insect. No right-minded trout would touch it. The solution to this problem is called a "leader."

FLY LINE TO LEADER

A leader is a tapered piece of nylon that is usually seven to nine feet long. At its thick end is a loop to which the heavy fly line can be attached. At the other end of the leader—its thin end—you can attach your fly. Since the nylon is translucent, a fly attached to it can appear to be alone and drifting freely.

The tip diameter of your leader should complement the size of the fly you are using. Large flies should be tied onto larger-diameter leader tips than smaller flies, which must be tied onto fine-tipped leaders. Only by properly matching fly size and leader-tip diameter can you expect to make aerodynamic casts through the air and realistic fly presentations on the water.

DIAMETER
CODE

1X	—	6 lb. TEST
2X	—	5 lb. TEST
3X	—	4 lb. TEST
4X	—	3 lb. TEST
5X	—	2 lb. TEST
6X	—	1 lb. TEST

1X

2X

3X

4X

5X

6X

NOTE- lb. TEST STRENGTHS ARE APPROXIMATE

Every time you cut off one fly and tie on another, you lose a few inches from the tip of your leader. If you change flies often, you can ruin a nice tapered leader in one day of fishing. To keep a leader intact, fly fishermen add a "tippet" to its end. A tippet is simply another piece of nylon that can be anywhere from one to three feet long. Tippets are added in keeping with the taper of the leader to which they are tied. For instance, if your leader ends in a three-pound-test tip, you would add a tippet of two-pound test. By carrying a few spools of tippet material, each a different pound test, you could add length to your leader while tapering it down. With only one basic leader, you could either cast large flies or, by adding tippets that taper down finer and finer, you could comfortably cast the tiniest flies.

Leader and tippet also serve to lengthen the distance between your fly and your fly line. The sight of a heavy fly line can frighten fish. This is particularly true in low-water streams and on quiet still water. For these fishing situations, the longer the leader, the better. The length of your leader can make the difference between scaring fish and catching them.

5X

4X

3X

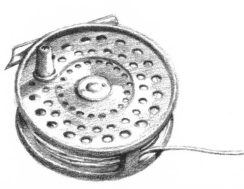

I had been fishing a still-water trout pond steadily for a week. Many flies were on the surface, and there were always some fish rising. Occasionally a large red-bellied brook trout would jump clear of the water. This should have been a fly fisherman's dream come true. For me it caused only frustration. The fish wouldn't come near any fly I offered. My casts were clean. My fly presentations were very natural. Yet every time I cast to a rising fish it seemed to be frightened away.

One day I met a gentleman who had caught his daily limit of trout. All of them were fly-fat brookies. We spoke about the pond and its trout. It turned out we were both using the same type of flies. While I was telling him of my frustration, he stared at my rod and line. Then, after taking his leave, he looked back at me and said, "Try a longer leader." I glanced at his. It must have been fifteen feet long!

Back in the water, I tied on a series of tippets, tapering them down as I lengthened my leader from ten to twelve feet. The sun was down. It was getting dark. I heard a big trout jump about thirty feet away and began a cast in the direction of the sound. My new longer leader carried the fly through the air, and I believed it had set down near the spot where the trout had surfaced. I strained my eyes to locate the floating fly in the darkness, but I couldn't see it. Then, with a loud *kerplunk!* the trout jumped up and grabbed the fly. For the next five minutes I stood in the dark holding my rod high and keeping the line taut as the heavy fish cut this way and that way through the black water, plunging deeper with each run. It was like being hooked to a submarine. All I could think of, from the time the fish took the fly to the moment I held it thrashing in my net, was that gentleman saying, "Try a longer leader."

THE FLY REEL

Most of the time your fly reel simply stores your line while you walk, wade, and fish. Your fly reel should be just big enough to hold your fly line, leader, and tippet plus approximately twenty-five yards of strong nylon backup line. The backup line is there in case you hook into a Moby Dick and it takes off with all of your fly line.

You do not reel in a fish with a fly reel; you reel in slack line. When playing a large fish, you reel in slack line as the fish allows it. While playing smaller fish, you do not reel in line at all. You pull in line a little at a time with your hand, letting it collect around you on the water. Then, after you have netted your fish, you reel in the loose line.

LINE GUARD
PROTECTS FLY LINE
FROM CHAFFING AS
IT IS BEING PULLED
FROM THE REEL.

4" DIA.
8-12 WT.
LINES

3½" DIA.
6-8 WT.
LINES

3" DIA.
2-6 WT.
LINES

FRONT

END

BACK

VENTILATING HOLES
ALLOW AIR TO DRY
WET FLY LINE
ON THE SPOOL.

DRAG CONTROL PUTS
PRESSURE ON THE
TURNING SPOOL TO
SLOW DOWN A FISH
THAT IS RAPIDLY PULLING
LINE OFF THE REEL.

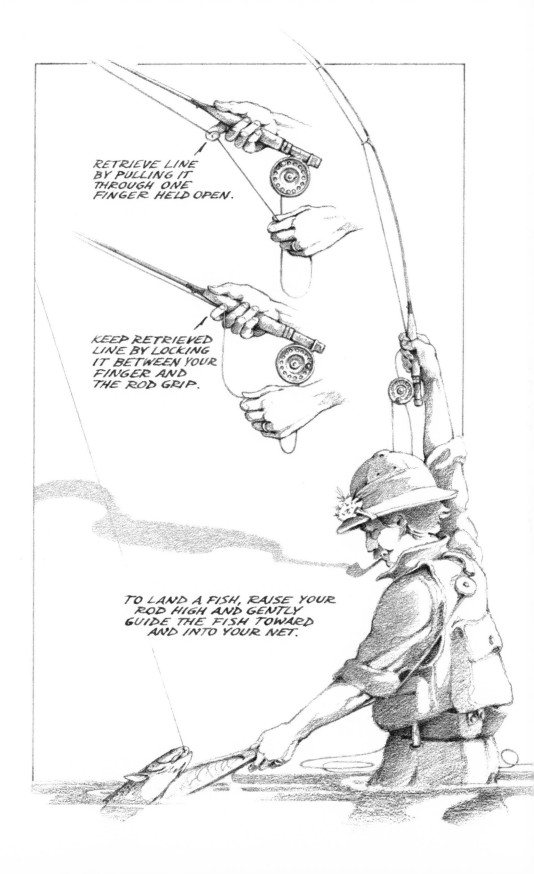

WINDINGS

FEMALE FERRULE

REEL SEAT

GRIP

FLY KEEPER

LINE GUIDES

FLY RODS

The fly rod is the instrument that makes casting a fly an act of beauty and grace. Fly rods are generally longer than other freshwater fishing rods. They are long so you can better control lengths of heavy fly line looping back and forth in the air during casting. They are long also to more accurately direct line to a desired spot on the water.

Every fly rod is marked on its butt section as to what weight fly line it was designed to be used with. There are fly rods that are built with just the right dynamics to properly cast a 2-weight fly line. There are fly rods made for casting a 3-weight fly line, fly rods for use with a 4-weight line, and so on. If you begin your fly-fishing with a "balanced" rod and line-weight combination, you will experience less frustration while learning to use it.

Fly rods also come in different lengths to suit a variety of fishing conditions. A medium-length fly rod (around seven and one-half to eight feet) will suit most fishing conditions in streams and ponds. Longer fly rods (nine feet and longer) are better for big open waters where powerful casts are often necessary. Long rods are also preferred by deep-wading fly fishers to help keep their line high and up off the water during backcasts. For the same

LONG ROD

SHORT ROD

MALE FERRULE

LINE GUIDES

reason long rods are used by those who fish from sitting positions in boats or float tubes. An extra-long rod is a boon in places where high banks or tall brush can foul your cast. When you buy a fly rod, consider the fishing conditions you will meet most often, and choose a rod length that will suit them.

There are fly rods made of fiberglass, of graphite, and of bamboo. The fiberglass rods are fine fishing rods. They are also inexpensive. My first fly rod, which I still own, is an eight-foot fiberglass rod for a 6-weight line. I learned how to cast with it. Graphite rods are a little more expensive than fiberglass rods. They are extremely light yet powerful. I have one of these beauties. It is nine and one-half feet long, and all business from butt to tip. Bamboo fly rods are beautiful to look at, exquisite to hold, and pure joy to fish with. They are also very expensive. Nevertheless, I wish every fly fisher could someday own one. I do most of my trout fishing with a bamboo fly rod made for a 6-weight line. Its bamboo has turned nut brown with the seasons. Its silk windings are wine red. The cork handle is sculptured to match the contours of my right hand's grip. This is more than a fishing rod. It is something of myself and my days astream that I can leave to my grandchildren.

LONG ROD

SHORT ROD

A CASTING LESSON

Remember, in fly fishing it is actually the special fly line that you cast to carry your leader, tippet, and fly out onto the water. So before you make any cast, be sure you have at least two feet of the fly line hanging out beyond the tip of your rod. This length of line will give you enough weight to flex your rod and begin your cast.

The basic fly fishing cast is one in which the line is first cast up and backward to build momentum for the cast forward. In this way of casting, you can add some distance to your cast by stripping a few feet of line from your reel as you begin your backcast. Then let it go shooting through the rod guides during your forward cast. During casting your fly reel serves only as a supply wheel from

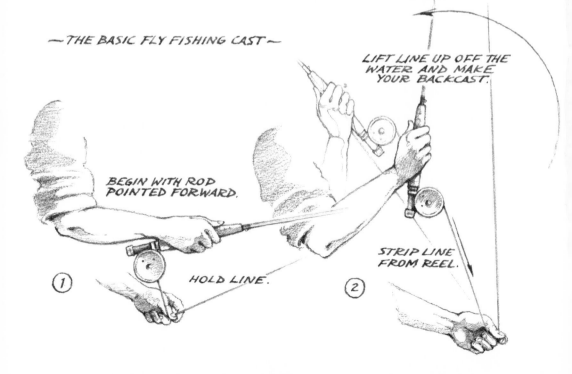

— THE BASIC FLY FISHING CAST —

LIFT LINE UP OFF THE WATER AND MAKE YOUR BACKCAST.

BEGIN WITH ROD POINTED FORWARD.

STRIP LINE FROM REEL.

HOLD LINE.

① ②

which you can strip lengths of line to throw into your cast. More and more casting distance can be gotten by keeping your line up in the air, looping back and forth in a series of "false casts"—using each subsequent backcast to strip additional shooting line from your reel. Then, when a desired casting distance is reached in a false cast, the line is backcast once more and finally cast forward onto the water.

In most streams and in ponds and lakes, fly casts of thirty feet are the average. If you fish up-current, in moving water, casting from a position behind your quarry, and if you practice stealth when fishing in still water, your casts can be even shorter. In trout brooks small enough to hop across, even a simple flip of your line may be too much of a cast. When I am fishing such fairy waters, I stalk each rill, pocket, and pool until I am close enough to simply reach out with my rod and swing a length of line—gently—to carry my fly to the spot I wish to fish.

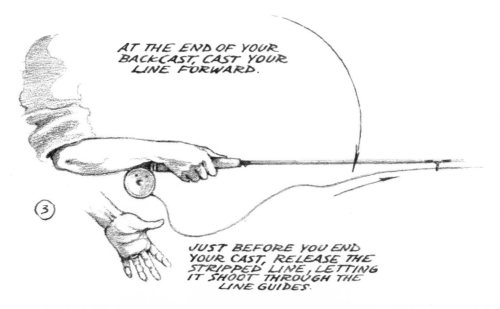

AT THE END OF YOUR BACKCAST, CAST YOUR LINE FORWARD.

③

JUST BEFORE YOU END YOUR CAST, RELEASE THE STRIPPED LINE, LETTING IT SHOOT THROUGH THE LINE GUIDES.

3
Walking and Wading

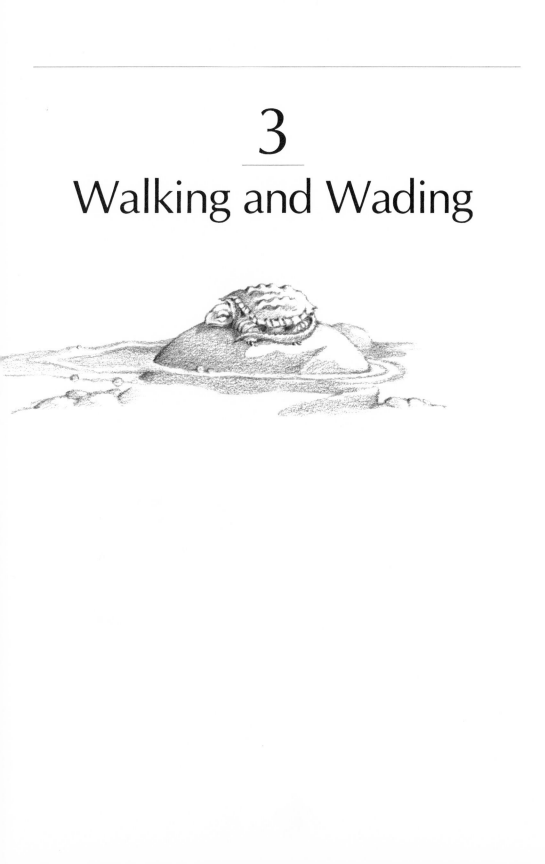

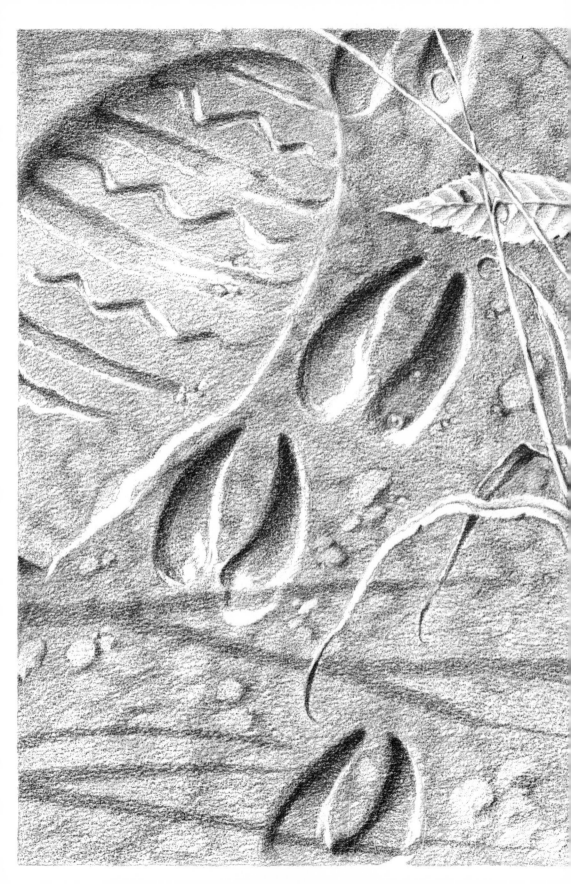

I was in the woods, following an old logging trail a friend had told me would lead to a stretch of our local river that I had never fished before. For a while it did seem that the trail was going to take me all the way to my destination, but it ended abruptly in a wide mushy gully. The river was still a long way off. There was a deer path in the sodden ground and I took advantage of it, stepping on hoofprints. Where the deer prints were less surefooted or were splayed, I placed my own feet cautiously. Some places were so marshy that I had to walk parallel to the trail, stepping only on matted clumps of grass to avoid sinking in the mud.

The path ended on the higher, harder ground of a long-neglected farm meadow. Here the grasses had grown wild to heights of five feet and more. As I pushed through the grass, small birds scattered ahead of me, silently winging between the stalks and blades. I came to a place where the meadow grass shared the soil with thistles, milkweed, and goldenrod. Pointing my fly rod forward, I threaded through the crowd. Over the heads of the plants I could see a wide meandering channel in the land. It was the river! I began to hurry, and my heavy steps startled a large snake, which startled me. Seeing the snake slowed me down. If it could feel the vibrations of my approach, the fish in the nearby water could too. Slowly, slowly, I stepped through giant ferns growing on the riverbank.

Crouching to avoid casting my shadow on the stream, I stalked the water for trout.

STALKING WATER

Fish are wild animals. Even those you may keep in a tank are wild and wary by nature. Fish of all species, from the time when they are little on up, are alert to any chance of being caught. Though they may grow to be lunker-sized, they retain their wariness. When you consider how many animals prey upon fish, this is not at all surprising. Otters, minks, fishers, raccoons, coyotes, foxes, humans, bears, muskrats, moles, eagles, ospreys, loons, grebes, herons, egrets, bitterns, sandpipers, gulls, screech owls, snakes, turtles, and even some spiders catch and eat freshwater fish. Even fish eat fish.

Most wild predators see the individual fish they are after. They wait for a fish to come close enough to nab, stalk a fish they see in shallow water, or dive underwater and swim after a fish. A person fishing, more often than not, does not see any fish until one inspects or takes the bait, lure, or fly. You cannot stalk fish you cannot see. You can, however, stalk the water. When you are fishing, you should come to every piece of water stalking, as if you were seeing fish in it and were actually stalking them. I try to remember this every time I'm out, but sometimes, in my excitement to begin fishing, I forget and plod in, frightening every fish in the area. When fish are frightened, they stop feeding. When fish are not feeding, you cannot catch them.

Before you reach the water, the fish in it can feel you coming. The vibrations of your footsteps travel through ground and water. When approaching still water, always walk slowly and softly. When you are nearing running water, stop before you reach it and listen. If you cannot hear the stream, take extra care not to approach with heavy steps. If you hear the stream running along noisily, you can be a bit more casual in your approach because any inadvertent sounds you may make will most likely be masked by the stream's own sound.

Many trout streams have free-stoned bottoms and banks. Loose stones make a sharp sound when knocked together. Every step you take on loose stones can produce a mixture of sharp clicking noises. These piercing sounds travel quickly through water and spook fish. When you are walking on loose stones, you cannot help making some noise, but you can limit it by walking along in slow motion, or by walking only a few steps, pausing awhile, then walking a few more steps, and so on until you reach your destination. A louder, more disturbing sound is created whenever you stand on a boulder that tilts under you and clunks down. Some boulders have a tendency to rock back and forth when you stand on them. They clunk this way, then that way, making two closely spaced noises. You can avoid creating this type of discord in the fishes' environment by stepping or standing only on boulders that are firmly in place.

AS YOUR WATER-STALKING SKILLS IMPROVE, YOUR GLIMPSES OF SHORELINE WILDLIFE WILL INCREASE.

NORTHERN WATER-THRUSH

Shadowed areas of a stream or pond attract fish, especially cold-water species, to the cool water there. Shadows moving above or over the water can frighten fish. Watch your shadow as you approach the water. As long as it remains cast on the ground, even the ground right up to the water's edge, the fish cannot notice it. If your shadow is cast on any vertical surface near or over the water—such as a high bank or rock or a stand of vegetation—it may be seen by fish as a threatening form. Never let your shadow fall on the water to which you are casting. A shadow cast on water happens twice, simultaneously—once across the surface and once along the bottom. If the water is shallow, with a calm flat surface, a shadow cast on it can be seen three times simultaneously—on the surface, on the bottom, and again in the bottom's reflection off the underside of the surface film. In shallow water, a fish may see one, two, or all three visions of a shadow's spooky presence and be frightened away.

Go fishing dressed in subdued colors that will blend with the natural surroundings of a stream or pond. At the water, if you are taller than the land forms or plant growth around you, conform to them by crouching to their average height. Anything you can do to disguise your human form and go unnoticed will help you catch fish.

WALKING IN WATER

There is something about the look, smell, sound, and feel of a body of water that is at once familiar and mysterious. Water, as much as fish, lures a fisherman. Fly fishers develop an intimacy with the waters in which they fish. They watch it intently, looking for insects and signs of feeding fish. Often they must wade in the water to stay away from shoreline brush and trees that would foul their looping casts.

When you are wading, move slowly, pushing gently through the water, and fish will not feel your presence. Take care to step quietly on the bottom, and fish will not hear you. Always stay far enough away from the spots to which you cast so the fish there will not see you in the water.

Fish in a stream usually face up-current, watching for drifting food. Since many of the currents in a stream flow in the same general direction as the

UPSTREAM APPROACH

CURRENT

mainstream, you can wade and fish upstream, knowing you will be approaching a number of fish from directly behind and out of their sight. An up-stream approach will also keep your scent, which will be flowing downstream from you, from reaching and possibly alerting the fish to which you are casting. In the pools and eddies of a stream there are always some currents that flow away from the mainstream or even flow in the opposite direction. When you are fishing such spots, try to distinguish the directions of the various currents flowing and cast up-current to each of them.

A quiet slow-wading person becomes a part of the watery environment, while all around, wild animals simply go about their business. One memorable day I saw a squadron of four merganser ducks swimming underwater in formation. They shot by, unaware of me, and sped together around the river's bend, staying underwater all the way.

I haven't waded or bumped into another crea-

FISH FACING
VARIOUS
CURRENTS

ture in the water, but I have come close. Turtles crawling weightlessly on the bottoms of streams have passed inches from my legs. Muskrats have paddled through the water toward me, coming so close that I was sure they would swim right into me. They never did.

The rule when wading is, Safety first—fishing last. Even if you are fishing with a friend, you are on your own in the water. Take each step carefully, making sure it will be firmly supported before taking another. If you step on bottom and feel no firmness at all, back off. Wade only far enough to be able to cast clear of shoreline vegetation. Usually, after wading only a few steps out, you can turn in the water and cast comfortably. Whatever type of wading gear you wear, hip boots or chest-high waders, remember they are not designed to be worn in water that is as deep as they are high on your body. Until I'm used to a place, I rarely wade into water over my knees. I never wade into water above my waist. In water above your waist, you become buoyant and are in less control of your body.

Each time I fish a spot, I wade in the exact places I've tried before and know to be safe. In unfamiliar water, I limit my wading to the very shallow, firm-bottomed areas. As I become more familiar with each visit to a place, I add to my mental walking map of safe, firm trails around and through the water.

Avoid wading where you cannot see the bottom clearly. In lakes and ponds there could be spring holes, beaver channels, and soft weed beds that you might sink into. There might be submerged objects to trip over, and sudden drop-offs where you could plunge deeply. Where there is water, there is erosion. Keep on the lookout for undermined shoreline trees that might fall and crumbling banks that could collapse.

Water is always deeper than it looks, and water current is always stronger than it appears on the surface. When wading streams, keep your body sideways to the flow to reduce your water resistance. Be careful when wading into any current that grows stronger as you go. The stronger the current, the deeper it cuts into the stream bed. If you feel a current becoming strong enough to push you over, move to a slower side of it.

When wading from one fishing spot to another, stay in the shallowest water near the shoreline. As you maneuver into a casting position, pause every few steps to look back and memorize the features of the water through which you have just passed, in case you have to retrace your steps to get back out. Then, as you continue onward, study the water features that lie ahead.

READING WATER

It takes time to really know a piece of water—to learn where the fish are and how you can wade safely to cast to them. The ability to look at a pond or a stream and tell what it may be like under its surface is called "reading water." In every body of water there are certain features or places that attract fish. When I find a new lake or pond, I spend a day hiking around its perimeter. I find out where it is shallow and where it looks deep. Fish in a lake or pond often go to the shallows to feed and to the depths to rest. I take note of rocky, weedy, muddy, and sandy places. All of these areas have edges where one place ends and another begins. Fish patrol these edges, hunting for food. I look for streams, rivulets, or springs flowing into the lake. On hot days fish often congregate in the cooler water these fresh water sources create as they mix into the pond. I remember those places where submerged tree trunks or stumps, sunken debris, and flooded structures like ancient stone walls or cellar holes could give fish refuge from open water. I once saw two bass, each easily weighing four pounds, swimming amid the flooded ruins of a stone building.

While I am reading the water, I am also on the lookout for landmarks to help me relocate the fish-

A LARGEMOUTH BASS HUNTING ALONG THE EDGE OF A WEED BED.

ing spots. I also watch for any animal tracks and wildlife signs—just for the pleasure of knowing who lives there.

Though a stream's surface may occasionally be flat and pondlike, its bottom never is. Fish are attracted to any change in the shape of a stream's bottom that creates the water conditions necessary to drift food to them. Under a flat stream surface there may be numerous hills and valleys. There may be long ridges, steep drops, or terraced levels. The bottom of a "flat-water" section of a stream may have many boulders, any one of which may be large enough for a good-sized fish to stay behind.

In a stream, wherever a boulder rests, a pocket of quiet water forms behind it. In the calm water of a "boulder pocket," a fish can watch for insects drifting in any of the currents flowing around the boulder and the perimeter of the pocket. If the boulder is large enough, a shallow depression forms in the stream bed directly in front of it where the impacting water digs under and around the boulder. Trout keeping to one side of a large boulder can watch the frontal depression for nymphs or caddis cases that have been caught in the swirl of sand and water.

In water reading there are three r's—rapids, runs, and riffles. All three can harbor fish—espe-

CURRENT

AN OVERVIEW OF A BOULDER POCKET SHOWING POSSIBLE FISH STATIONS.

CURRENT

FRONTAL DEPRESSION

cially species with streamlined bodies such as trout and salmon. How even these fish hold their own against the relentless, surging power of a rapids is a wonder. Yet I have seen even small trout—leaping rainbows—slice forward through a rapids, their slim backs black and shiny against the white-water bubbles.

STREAM RUN

A stream "run" is exactly that. It is where the water takes off in a direct run. A run in a stream will often appear slightly darker than the surrounding water color. This is because runs, by nature, have more water volume and can cut more deeply into the stream bed. Fish may choose to stay in the upper water of a run, near the surface, where they can snatch any insects that are floating quickly by. Fish may hold in the middle of a run where the current is fastest and strongest but also providing. And fish may lie deep in a run where the friction caused by the stream bed slows the current down. There, hugging bottom, under the protection of the upper current, a trout can nymph day and night.

In a stony stream where the water is shallow, it "riffles" over the lumps and bumps of the bottom. Riffles are my favorite places in a stream. They are happy-looking spots and the sound of riffling water reminds me of people joking and laughing. Riffles are also places favored by trout. The shallow, easygoing water provides just the right conditions for insect life. In riffles there are also plenty of sub-merged-boulder pockets where trout can rest.

As shallow as the water in a riffling stream is, you cannot see the trout living in it. This is why many beginning anglers bypass riffles. They look over the stream bottom, and because they see no fish, they move on. But, however colorful fish are out of water, in it they are only a variation of the water's color. Trout holding in riffles blend so per-fectly with the slender stones and strands of vege-tation on the stream bottom, they are virtually invisible. When a trout suddenly leaps or rolls over on the surface after a floating fly or slashes side-ways in the water to take a drifting nymph, the light hitting it broadside momentarily exposes it.

A stream pool is a body of water within a body of water. The different currents flowing into, around, through, and out of a pool form distinct areas known as the pool's "parts." The parts of a pool, from upstream down, are: head, middle, tail, and lip. The head of a pool is where the water first flows in from upstream. A pool is always deepest at or near its head because the entering water wears or scoops out a depression in the stream bed. The middle of a pool is where the water collects over the depression and stalls momentarily before moving along. The tail of a pool

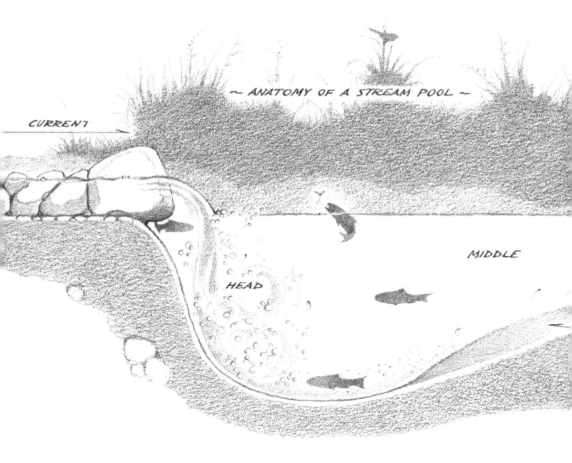

CURRENT

~ ANATOMY OF A STREAM POOL ~

MIDDLE

HEAD

is the stretch of water leaving the middle of the pool. The water in the tail of a pool becomes progressively shallower as it trails off toward the lip, at the very end of the pool, where it exits and continues its journey downstream. Fish may be in any one or in all of the parts of a pool. Whenever I discover a stream pool, I linger there as the water lingers. I take time to fish all of its parts individually, beginning with the lip, moving upstream to the tail, then casting to the middle, and finally trying my luck at the head.

TAIL OF POOL

LIP

SHOAL OF SAND
OR GRAVEL
EXCAVATED
FROM HEAD.

When you are fishing and come to a bend in the stream, pause and study the water coming into, swirling around, and running out of the turn. All of the currents can be carrying food, and fish will be stationed along them somewhere, watching and waiting. Approach every stream bend with the understanding that any place in it, not just the deepest spot, can hold fish—and lots of them.

Not far from our farm is a stream bend I call the "Cornfield Bend" because just where the water turns, it cuts into the edge of a cornfield. The Cornfield Bend is a wonderful example of how one small place in a stream can support many fish. The water flows into the bend after being slowed by a brief section of sunken tree trunks, railroad ties, and fence posts. Washed downstream by previous floods, these are now snagged together and firmly lodged in the bottom. Trout, brookies and browns, live in the holes and alleyways created by the debris. Right after the last of the sunken trunks, the stream makes a sharp right turn, and the outside curve of the turn digs into the sandy soil of the cornfield. There, the water digs deeply into the bank. The undercut looks dark and mysterious. There are some large brown trout living under the bank. Also living there, in the deep water, are suckers, chubs, and perch.

On the inside of the bend, the bottom slopes

ever-so-gently. Small brook trout stay on the upper part of the slope, where the water is less than a foot deep. For these fish, a trip to the surface after a bug and back is only a somersault. All down the slope, at various degrees of depth, are more trout—some brookies, some browns, and an occasional rainbow. They face the gentle currents on the sandy slope, watching for food that drifts over the bright granules. The Cornfield Bend ends in a short but energetic run along a clay ledge. There are always some trout holding deep in the run and more higher up, keeping in the shade under the ledge.

CURRENT

~THE CORNFIELD BEND~

SUNKEN TIMBER

INSIDE SLOPE

UNDERCUT BANK

CLAY LEDGE

CORNFIELD

4

Watching for Fish

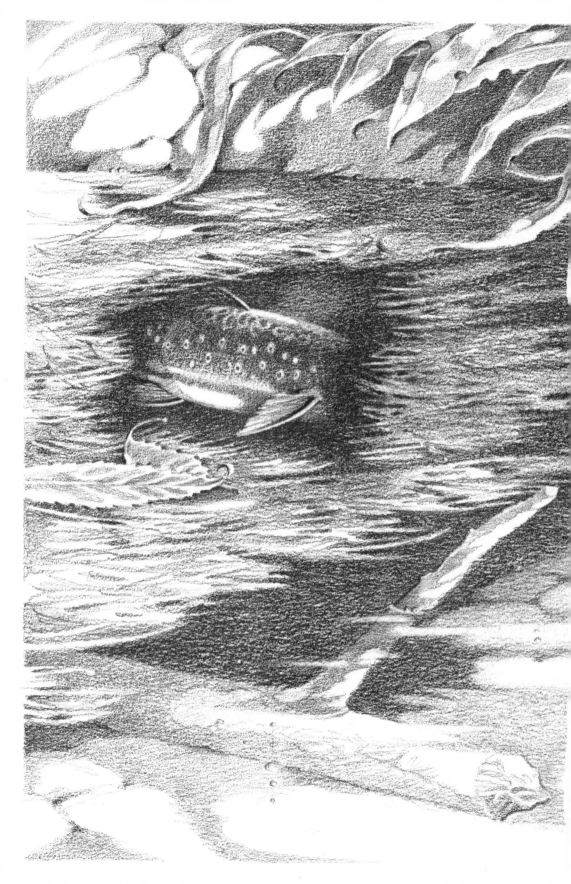

In one of the small backwater pools in a beaver's pond I watched a lone trout swimming. It was a male brookie, vivid in its autumn spawning colors. It cruised over the pool's dark bottom of sunken, rotting leaves and under brilliant, new-fallen leaves floating on the pool's surface. Every so often, the trout would bump or nudge its nose against some little piece of debris drifting in the water. Once it rose and sipped something in the surface film, something so small I could not see it.

The fish began to travel around the edge of the pond exploring every impression and crevice in the bank. It would swim out of sight under part of the bank, then reappear a foot or so farther on. At one point it disappeared under a floating shelf of dropped pine needles. It was black-looking under there, and for some time the fish did not come out. There was a small opening in the needles through which light poured, and I glimpsed the trout as it swam by in the water. When the fish finally left the shade of the pine needles, it passed, like a shadow itself, over a sunlit bar of gravel. Then it turned, flashing briefly but brightly, and headed out of the pool toward the main pond.

Any object that touches a water surface, whether it is a raindrop hitting it from above or a sunfish kissing it from below, creates a water ring that widens until it dissipates. On choppy, wavy, or rippling water these rings are difficult to see, but they will be there wherever anything touches the surface. On flat water, surface rings are obvious. They are often the only water disturbances that you see. I cast to every water ring, though I know it could have been made by a rising newt, a tadpole, or even by air breathed up from the bottom. To me, any ring on the water whispers, "Fish."

Strong broadly widening water rings are nearly always signs of rising fish. In the center of a rise ring there could be a clue as to whether the fish has risen to take a floating insect off the surface or a swimming insect just below the surface. When a fish sips an insect down off the surface, it gets a gulp of air too. This air is expelled immediately, and it returns to the surface trapped in a single water bubble. The water bubble emerges right in the center of the rise ring. A fish taking something under the surface gulps no air. There is no bubble in the center of its rise ring. This bit of information is important to fly fishing because if the fish are feeding on the surface, a floating dry-fly is used. If the fish are feeding below the surface, a sinking wet-fly is used.

SOME COMMON RISEFORMS TO LOOK FOR

PHANTOM RISE
[V-SHAPED WAVE]

SIPPING
RISE

GULPING
RISE

A BUBBLE IN THE CENTER OF A RISE-RING SUGGESTS AN INSECT HAS BEEN TAKEN THAT WAS FLOATING ON THE WATER SURFACE.

Any motion of a fish rising toward, coming near, or pushing through the water surface is called a "riseform." There are riseforms in which the fishes' bodies remain submerged and obscure. Only the dimples, bulges, swirls, spritzes, or splashes they create on the water surface (along with their accompanying water rings) are visible. In other riseforms the fishes' bodies can be seen surfacing—poking, humping, rolling, or leaping out of the water.

If a riseform is subtle, barely disturbing the water surface and creating only a tiny water ring, it does not necessarily mean that the fish making it is small. Large trout, especially browns, are noted for their dainty, dimpling rises. Smallmouth bass, from fingerlings to "armlings," take a floating fly with hardly a bother to the water surface.

LEAPING RISE

ROLL-OVER RISE

TAIL-SLAPPING RISE

HUMPING RISE

LUNGING RISE

I was fishing along the shoreline of a forest pond. I couldn't see any insects on the water and had been casting a large "attractor" fly with little luck. While looking at the very shallow water along the shore, I noticed a tiny surface dimple appear and disappear. I cast my fly to the spot and immediately a tiny dimple formed around it. Anxiously I raised my rod and pulled the fly away. Another dimple formed in the same spot on the water. Could it be a tiny perch, rising repeatedly? I cast again to the spot, and again a dimple formed around my fly. Suddenly I felt the powerful surge of a large fish pulling my line through the water. The dimpler was not a perch. It was a big bruiser of a bass. The fish took off on a rod-bending run, at the end of which it leaped up through the surface, somersaulted in the air, and belly flopped back down to run some more. A nearby fisherman exclaimed at the sight and others began talking as they watched the bass pulling my rod tip down closer and closer to the water.

After about three minutes of running, diving, and jerking, the bass surfaced again. This time it rocketed straight up into the air, tail-walked across the surface, and then dove into the water. Fishermen were migrating from their own fishing spots, some on foot, some in boats, to get a closer look. Among them I could hear a low voice saying,

"Keep it down! Keep it in the water!" If a fish you are playing jumps too often, it can eventually break free.

After five minutes of playing the heavy fish, my right wrist and arm were getting tired. I held the rod handle against my chest with both hands as the bass cannonballed over the boulder-strewn pond bottom, pulling nearly all the line off my reel. Then it began to slow down and I retrieved line little by little as it slackened. When both of us were exhausted, I pulled the fish to me. Nearly ten minutes from the moment it sipped down my fly, I lifted the bass out of the water. That fish, my friends, was a keeper!

Great bulging riseforms can only be made by big fish. The sight of one of these rises in the water can curl your toes inside your waders. A bulging riseform is a sign that there are nymphs swimming to the surface to emerge. The bulge on the water surface is created by the humping back or arching side of a fish as it gobbles up the swimming insects. Very often, fish feeding this way will hump up or roll over right through the surface and you can see them showing out of the water. I am reminded of the many rainbow trout I have seen rolling over on the surface—their glistening sides flashing pink and silver in the sunlight. If the emerging insects are abundant, the fish surface again and again, sometimes waving their tails in satisfaction.

SWIRLING RISEFORM

When a fish rushes up and snatches something near or on the surface, then quickly turns and scoots back to where it was, it creates a swirling riseform. Most of the times I have seen a swirling riseform, the fish making it was taking some large prey such as a giant species of nymph or fly, a meaty terrestrial, or a swimming frog or mouse. I once watched a trout swirl around a swimming mouse, grab hold of the mouse's front end, and then have the devil of a time getting the rest of the mouse underwater. The mouse's hind end was up and out of the water. Its long tail expressed the fear and panic of the situation—waving, curling, and shaking in the air. When the trout began jerking the mouse around the surface, trying harder to pull it under, the mouse's tail became erect. It looked almost as though the mouse were pushing with its hind feet and legs against the fish's head, trying desperately to pull free. But the trout was determined. Its jaws were clamped tight. It dragged the mouse across the stream to a place near a submerged log, and there the struggle ended when the trout finally brought the mouse down. A small circle of water bubbles briefly marked the surface spot.

5
Fishing with Flies

It was early evening. The trout in the Cornfield Bend were feeding on the surface. Wading slowly upstream toward them, I heard a deep warbling sound. At first I took it to be some river bird singing its late-day song. Then I recognized the ascending notes of the musical scale. Somewhere a clarinetist was beginning to practice, and the woodwind tones were traveling down the valley.

By the time I had waded close enough to be casting my fly to the rising trout, the musician was playing a classical piece. The notes were clear and flowing like the water. I imagined a piping Pan sitting cross-hooved on the bank, hidden by the summer foliage. The river flowed. The fish rose. The player played. It was an enchanting mixture of sight and sound, and I was casting in its spell—waving and pointing my bamboo wand—making trout appear at the touch of a feathered fly on the water.

USING DRY-FLIES

There is always a touch of magic in catching a fish with a surface fly. Your fly alights on the water and floats. Now you see it—now you don't. A fish has sipped it down. You cast to a spot on the water where you know a fish to be, but you do not see it. Now you do. It leaps to take your fly!

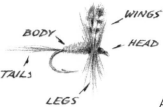

BODY

WINGS

HEAD

TAILS

LEGS

Any fishing fly designed to float on the water is called a "dry-fly." There are dry flies tied to look like mayfly duns and mayfly spinners, some that copy caddisflies, others resembling stoneflies, and more that pass as mosquitos, gnats, and midges. Grasshoppers, crickets, beetles, bees, ants, and other terrestrials also have dry-fly counterparts. All dry-flies are tied on very lightweight wire hooks. Their bodies are made of water resistant materials. Their tails, if they have them, are stiff, and the hackle feathers used to suggest their legs and wings are wound thick and bushy. All of these features help keep dry-flies sitting high and dry, propped up on the water's surface.

During use, even the best-tied dry-flies will eventually become waterlogged and sink. Usually a few crisp false casts are enough to air-dry a soaked fly so it will float again. Some fly fishers use a commercial "fly floatant" to dress each dry-fly before they begin fishing with it. This additional waterproofing can help keep a fly dry and buoyant for hours of fishing.

When flies are floating on or flying above the water and fish are rising after them, try to match the natural insect in size, color, and type (if you have it) with a dry-fly of your own and cast it to a spot where you saw a fish rising. When there are no insects on the water and no sign of fish, fishing

CARRY YOUR DRY-FLIES IN A BOX
THAT HAS ROOM ENOUGH FOR
LOTS OF BUSHY HACKLES.

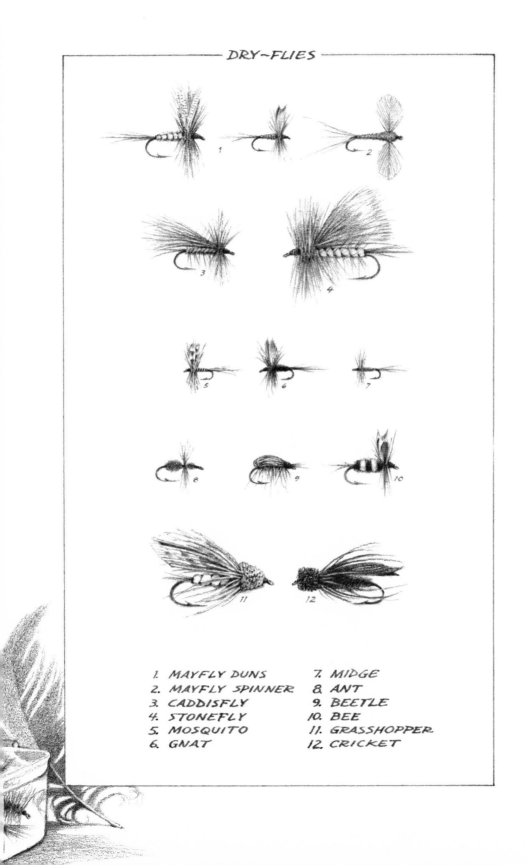

1. MAYFLY DUNS
2. MAYFLY SPINNER
3. CADDISFLY
4. STONEFLY
5. MOSQUITO
6. GNAT
7. MIDGE
8. ANT
9. BEETLE
10. BEE
11. GRASSHOPPER
12. CRICKET

CURRENT →

KEEP YOUR ROD
POINTED
TOWARD YOUR
DRIFTING FLY.

a dry-fly is impractical but still possible. You can try to attract a fish by casting a big "buggy" fly to promising-looking spots.

On still water, a floating fly can be thoroughly inspected by a fish before the fish either rejects or accepts it. A fish may inspect your fly once, reject it and swim away, then return to look it over again and take it. So whenever you cast a dry-fly onto a pond, lake, or even a quiet stream pool, let it float for as long as your patience will allow. You can never tell what might be eyeballing the fly from below.

To fish a dry-fly on moving water, cast to a point upstream from a rising fish or fish-holding spot and let your fly float downstream over it. A dry-fly floating with a current may be seen by a number of fish and could stimulate any one of them into taking it. All the while your fly is floating, watch for a slap, smack, swirl, or splash—any sign of a rising fish near it. Follow your fly's downstream progress with your rod and be ready to raise its tip to set the

CAST

DRIFT

CURRENT

A FISH MAY LEAVE ITS POST
AND FOLLOW YOUR DRIFTING
FLY TO INSPECT IT A WHILE
BEFORE TAKING IT.

hook the moment a fish strikes. Once a floating dry-fly comes to the end of its drift and begins to drag on the water, no fish will touch it. That is the time to pick it up and make a fresh cast.

Fish will jump right out of the water into the air when they are after slow-flying duns just leaving the surface; egg-laying mayflies, caddisflies, and stoneflies skipping over or dipping down to the water; and many other airborne insects that they see. I have also seen fish leap out of the water to catch emerging caddisflies that have just popped to the surface. The fish rush up to catch the flies quickly, and it is each fish's own momentum that carries it beyond its mark into the air.

Fish often miss a moving target. I saw a small brook trout jump out of the water after an egg-laying stonefly that was hovering inches above the surface. The brookie couldn't have had a bigger or easier target. Yet it missed the stonefly completely and, what was worse, tumbled over and landed smack in the water on its back!

END OF DRIFT
DRAG

IF A FISH SEES YOUR FLY DRAGGING ON THE SURFACE, IT WILL LOSE INTEREST AND RETURN TO ITS POST.

USING WET-FLIES

Many dry-fly patterns have wet-fly counterparts. Whereas dry-flies generally represent completely emerged winged insects, their wet-fly counterparts suggest the insects in an earlier stage, as they are swimming up to the surface to emerge. There are wet-fly patterns that suggest swimming mayflies, stoneflies, caddisflies and their pupae, and the pupae of mosquitos, gnats, and midges. There are also wet-flies that imitate drowning ants.

Since wet-flies are supposed to be fished underwater, they are tied on heavy wire hooks to make them sink. And since all wet-flies are best fished full of motion, any wings, hackles, and tails are soft and flexible so they will undulate and be lifelike in the water. Because of the action that anglers give them, wet-flies provoke fish. Strikes are fast and hard.

To fish a wet-fly in moving water, cast slightly upstream and let the fly drift by you, floating downstream with the current. If a fish takes the fly during this "dead" drift, be quick to raise your rod and set the hook. When the fly comes to the end of its drift, it will swing around and hold steady in the current. This swinging about-face is particularly exciting to fish because it duplicates the motion of a fast-emerging insect. Be prepared for an

WET-FLIES
WHEN WET
LOOK FLESHY
AND ALIVE.

CAST

DRIFT AND SINK

CURRENT

END OF DRIFT
SWING

"SWIMMING" RETRIEVE

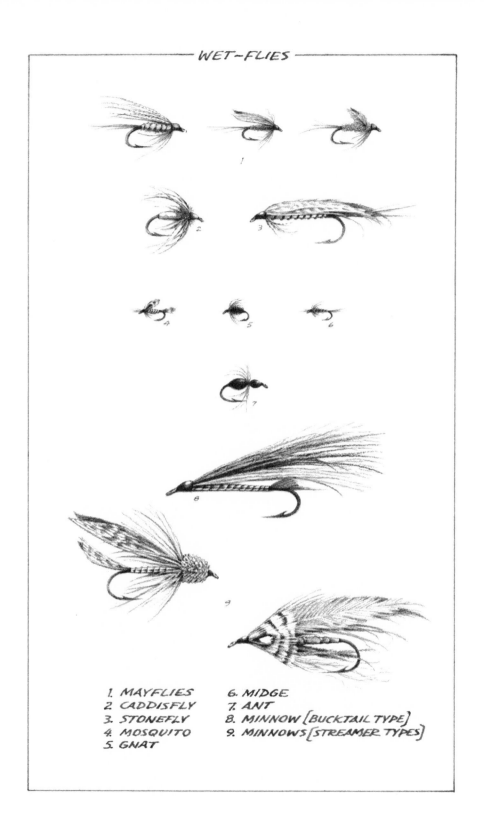

1. MAYFLIES   6. MIDGE
2. CADDISFLY   7. ANT
3. STONEFLY   8. MINNOW (BUCKTAIL TYPE)
4. MOSQUITO   9. MINNOWS (STREAMER TYPES)
5. GNAT

enthusiastic strike. If you get none, begin jerking your rod back every few seconds to make the fly dart enticingly against the current. If that doesn't produce a fish, start "swimming" the fly upstream, back to you, by hand-retrieving line.

Very small wet-flies should be retrieved no more than six inches at a time to make them look like tiny swimming insects. Retrieve larger wet flies a foot or so with each pull, stopping every so often to make the fly pause naturally as a real insect might, to rest between spurts of action.

A
BLACK-NOSED
DACE
AND ITS BUCKTAIL
COUNTERPART.

Any wet-fly, large or small, cast onto the still water of a pond or lake, will float until it becomes waterlogged. Then it will sink steadily, all the way to the bottom if you let it. As soon as you begin retrieving the fly, it will stop descending and start angling upward with your pulls. So, if you want to fish a wet-fly just under the surface of a pond, begin retrieving it as soon as it starts to sink. To fish a wet-fly more deeply, wait some seconds after it has sunk before you begin your retrieve. As always, be alert for a fish to grab your fly anywhere along the way back to you. When you have retrieved all but a few feet of your fly line, pick your leader, tippet, and fly up out of the water and cast again to begin another fishing cycle.

The large flies fishermen call "streamers" and "bucktails" are essentially wet-flies that are tied specifically to imitate minnows. They are fished the same ways wet-flies are, retrieved with erratic, minnowlike darts. The very first fly I ever used was a big bucktail. I hooked my first trout on it. I was standing in a cold mountain brook wearing, not waders, but a pair of knee-high Indian moccasins. I cast the bucktail onto the water and let it drift a little way downstream over a small falls and into the middle of a shallow pool. There, at the end of my line, the fly held, facing upstream. It looked just like a slender minnow waving its tail in the water. I jerked my rod back once to make the bucktail dart as though it were trying to swim against the current and, in a silvery flash, the fly was seized by a large brook trout. Instinctively, I raised my rod, setting the hook, and the fish went berserk.

I began retrieving lengths of line, pulling the wild fighting trout upstream toward me a foot at a time until, finally, it was thrashing and splashing in the water around my soggy moccasins. Then, as I was reaching down with my net to scoop my prize from the brook, the fish broke free and shot away. I was left trembling with excitement and for the next minutes only that trout—its black back and speckled sides, its glistening head and shining eyes, its fins, its tail—all its lively image—swirled in my mind.

NYMPH FISHING

FLY-SINKING PASTES,
LIKE FLY-FLOATANTS,
COME IN SMALL
CONTAINERS THAT
CAN BE PINNED
TO A SHIRT OR VEST.

JUST A DAB
OF PASTE ON
YOUR FLY WILL
MAKE IT SINK.

Down on the rocky bottoms of cold-water streams, trout feed day and night, in fair weather or foul, and in all seasons, on nymphs. The fish find nymphs that are clinging to or crawling on the stones. They grub for nymphs that are burrowing under sand or silt. They watch the water to catch nymphs they see swimming or tumbling in the currents. If you were a trout, you would be probably munching, swallowing, or digesting a nymph right now. Fly fishermen who have the patience to bump an artificial nymph along the bottom of a stream often catch more and bigger fish than others using wet-flies or dry-flies. There are a number of ways to get a nymph all the way down on the bottom, even in a strong current. The fly can be originally "weighted," that is, tied on a hook that has had some wire wrapped around its shank before the body of the fly was spun. An unweighted nymph can be pulled down under by a split-shot sinker or two squeezed onto the tippet a foot or so above the fly. Or you can smear a nymph with some commercial fly-sinking paste. These pastes are harmless to fish and people. I always use paste first. If that doesn't get the nymph down quickly enough, I squeeze a split-shot onto the tippet. If that doesn't do the job I squeeze on another, then another, and so on.

BE SURE TO SQUEEZE SPLIT-SHOT
TIGHTLY ONTO YOUR LINE. LOST
LEAD SINKERS ARE HARMFUL TO
THE FISH AND BIRDS THAT FIND
AND EAT THEM.

ADD SPLIT-SHOT
ONLY AS YOU NEED
THEM.

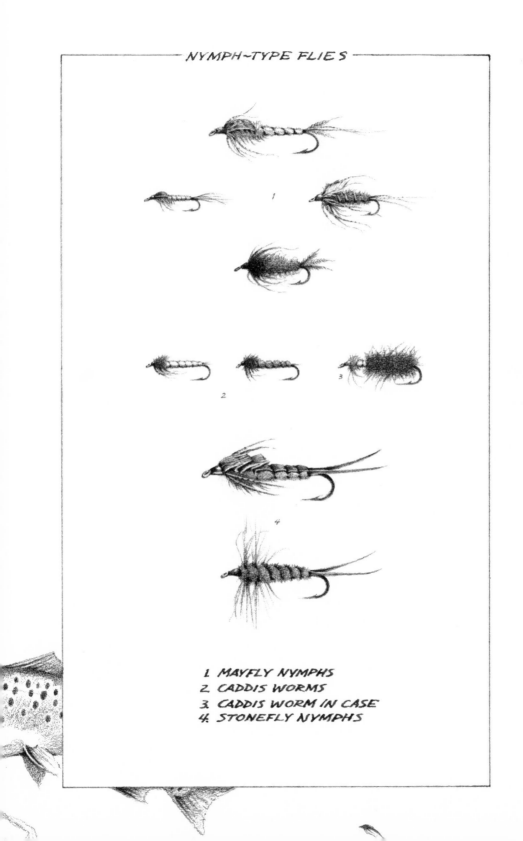

1. MAYFLY NYMPHS
2. CADDIS WORMS
3. CADDIS WORM IN CASE
4. STONEFLY NYMPHS

Casting such weight with a fly rod is cumbersome. Be careful not to let the fly swing down and hook your hat, or worse, your ear. Cast your nymph with a slow overhand lob upstream as far as you can. After the fly has sunk, hold your rod high, keeping all the slack out of your line. You should be able to feel the split-shot bumping or dragging on the stream's bottom. Your nymph will be tumbling along behind it. All this time, your floating fly line will be drifting just a little faster than your nymph is moving down below. So, even though you cannot see your fly, you can estimate its location underwater. It will always be a few feet farther upstream than your line tip. Watch that line tip carefully. It is your fish indicator. If it pauses—raise your rod higher and strike to set the hook in case you have a fish. If your line tip begins to move in any new direction—even slightly—strike. If it twitches—strike. If your line stops drifting completely—strike! Whenever your nymph has come to the end of its downstream drift, make it

A FISH CAUGHT ON ANY FLY,
WHETHER NYMPH, WET, OR DRY,
IS MOST LIKELY TO BE HOOKED
ONLY IN ITS LIP. ANY FISH YOU
CHOOSE TO RELEASE CAN BE
EASILY UNHOOKED AND, IF HANDLED
GENTLY, SET FREE VIRTUALLY
UNHARMED.

WITH A NARROW PLIERS
YOU CAN BEND
DOWN THE BARB ON
YOUR FLY TO INSURE
EASY UNHOOKING.

swim back upstream exactly as you would a wet-fly of comparable size.

Artificial nymphs need not always be fished weighted and on the bottom, nor just in streams. I particularly enjoy fishing unweighted nymphs in ponds and lakes. You can make them swim out in open water as though they were migrating. Or they can be fished just under the water surface as though they were struggling through the surface film to emerge. I began to fish nymphs suspended in the film, motionless, like recently evacuated shucks, after catching perch, bass, and trout whose mouths and throats were jammed full of nothing but shucks.

Fishing nymphs on the calm surface of a pond or a lake can have all the visual excitement of dry-fly fishing, and sometimes, even more. When great hordes of small still-water nymphs are emerging, big fish often cruise just under the surface film gorging themselves. I have often been fishing when large trout were feeding in this way. Watching an individual feeding fish's slow progress as it moves along, rising repeatedly, can be fascinating.

SURFACE PROGRESS OF
A NYMPH-GORGING TROUT.

One moment you may see only the fish's dorsal fin knife through the surface. You may see its wide tail waving out of the water or its broad back humping up. Waiting as a big fish cruises nearer and nearer, until it is close enough for you to cast your own nymph into its feeding path, and then seeing that fish take your fly in a great bulging riseform, are among the most suspenseful and thrilling experiences a fly fisher can have.

Fly fishing keeps you watching water, wondering and excited about the life in it. Whether you are crawling along the mossy bank of a mountain brook, wading in its clear cold water, or holding one of its colorful trout in your hands, you are in touch with the natural world.